Winter Warnings

The 2024 UK Snow Forecast and Weather Patterns

Gary D. Bryant

Copyright

Copyright © [2024] by Gary D. Bryant

All rights reserved. No part of this book may be reproduced or transmitted in any form or by any means, electronic or mechanical, including photocopying, recording, or by any information storage and retrieval system, without permission in writing from the publisher,except for the inclusion of brief quotations in a review.

Table of Contents

Chapter 1: Understanding the 2024 Winter Outlook and prediction for the UK   **5**

Chapter 2: Staying Updated on Winter Warnings   **14**

Chapter 3: How Snow and Winter Conditions Impact Daily Life   **22**

Chapter 4: Staying Safe in Severe Winter Conditions   **29**

Chapter 5: How to Prepare for Snow and Freezing Temperatures   **34**

Introduction:

As winter draws closer, UK residents are once again keeping a close eye on the weather forecast. Predictions of snow showers, Arctic blasts, and high-pressure systems have stirred curiosity about what lies ahead in the coming months. Based on early reports from the Met Office, November is expected to bring a mix of chilly air, frost, and the possibility of snow showers in northern and eastern areas.

This book dives into the UK's winter weather trends for 2024, from the science behind Arctic blasts to regional predictions on snowfall and freezing temperatures. By exploring forecasts and patterns, Winter Warnings offers readers a clearer understanding of what to expect and how to prepare for this year's cold season. As you follow along, you'll gain insights into how shifting pressures, temperatures, and moisture levels come together to shape the UK's unique winter climate.

Chapter 1: Understanding the 2024 Winter Outlook and prediction for the UK

Chapter Overview

In this chapter, we'll explore the key weather predictions for the upcoming winter season in the UK. Drawing on insights from the Met Office and other leading forecasters, we'll break down expected temperature shifts, potential snowfall areas, and the driving forces behind this year's winter weather patterns.

Expected Conditions and Timeline

The Met Office's winter forecast for 2024 points toward notable weather shifts as early as late October. Forecasts indicate a likely mix of settled periods and sudden cold snaps, especially in northern and eastern UK regions. Here's a closer look at what to anticipate month-by-month:

Late October: Milder weather with scattered rain, but colder air beginning to move in from the north.

Early November: High pressure could usher in colder conditions, especially in northern Scotland, with potential snow showers in elevated areas.

Mid-November to December: Below-average temperatures may increase the chance of widespread frost and fog, with snow most likely in northern highlands and other higher altitudes.

Main Weather Influences

Arctic Air: Cold air from the Arctic is expected to move into the UK, especially in northern and eastern areas. This cold air, combined with high pressure, may lead to freezing temperatures, frost at night, and occasional light snow.

High Pressure: High-pressure systems generally bring settled, cold weather. Clear skies at night can increase frost chances, but the exact position of these systems will affect whether we stay cold or get some milder weather.

Jet Stream: The jet stream, which influences storm paths across the Atlantic, is expected to dip south, allowing cold Arctic air to reach the UK. This could increase the chance of early snow in some areas.

Regional Impact

Northern UK: Scotland, northern England, and Northern Ireland may bear the brunt of early snowfall and colder conditions. In these areas, temperatures may drop below freezing, with snow potentially accumulating on higher ground.

Southern and Central UK: Milder conditions are expected in southern and central parts, although brief cold snaps and morning frosts are possible as the season progresses.

Regional breakdown

Scotland: Scotland, especially the Highlands and northern areas, may get early snow because of its closeness to Arctic air and its mountains. Temperatures could drop to freezing or below, with snow possibly starting in early November.

Northern England: Higher places like the Pennines and Lake District are more likely to see snow. Cold air moving south from Scotland could bring snow to these areas, especially when high pressure is present in early November.

Northern Ireland: While early snow is less likely, Northern Ireland might still get occasional snow in the western and northern areas when colder air moves in.

Factors Influencing Regional Snowfall

Several factors affect where snow is likely to fall, including altitude, temperature patterns, and regional proximity to the Arctic:

Altitude: Higher altitudes tend to be colder and are more likely to accumulate snow, especially during early winter.

Latitude: The farther north a region, the closer it is to Arctic air, increasing the likelihood of snow and colder temperatures.

Proximity to the Coast: Coastal areas typically have milder temperatures due to the ocean's influence, making them less prone to early snow, though inland areas may still experience colder, snowy conditions.

Key Takeaways

The UK may experience an earlier and colder winter this year, with the possibility of snowfall in the northern regions.

Arctic air masses, high-pressure systems, and the jet stream are key influencers of these predictions.

Preparation and staying informed are essential to navigate the challenges of winter weather.

Chapter 2: Staying Updated on Winter Warnings

Chapter Overview

In this chapter, we'll explore the importance of staying informed about winter weather warnings, especially during an unsettled season. Understanding and preparing for alerts issued by the Met Office and other weather services can help ensure safety, whether you're at home, commuting, or planning any outdoor activities. This chapter will guide you on how to stay updated and respond to various winter weather warnings effectively.

Understanding Winter Weather Warnings

The UK's winter weather can be unpredictable, with sudden shifts in conditions like heavy snow, ice, and fog. The Met Office provides warnings to help the public prepare, issuing alerts that range from mild advisories to severe warnings. Here's a quick overview of the warning levels:

Yellow Warning: Alerts people to be cautious, as weather may disrupt daily activities. For instance, light snow may cause minor delays in transportation.

Amber Warning: Calls for people to be prepared for possible impacts. This warning suggests a higher likelihood of disruption due to more intense weather, like heavy snow or freezing rain.

Red Warning: The most severe warning level, advising people to take immediate action. Dangerous weather conditions are expected, posing a high risk to life and property.

By understanding these levels, you'll know when to make travel changes, prepare for potential power outages, or take other protective steps.

How to Stay Updated on Winter Weather

To stay on top of winter weather changes, especially during unsettled periods, there are several reliable sources and tools available:

Met Office Website and App: The Met Office provides real-time weather forecasts and detailed maps. Their app also offers customizable alerts, allowing you to receive updates specific to your region.

Social Media: Following the Met Office on Twitter, Facebook, and other social platforms gives you quick access to urgent updates. Many local councils also share relevant weather updates, especially for local road conditions and emergency responses.

Local News Channels and Radio: Broadcasting reliable weather forecasts and updates, local news channels provide essential information on any road closures, power outages, or disruptions.

National Severe Weather Warning Service (NSWWS): The NSWWS is a service run by the Met Office that sends out alerts for severe weather, enabling you to be prepared for conditions that might significantly impact your area.

Weather Apps and Websites: In addition to the Met Office, other apps like BBC Weather and Weather.com can offer different perspectives on the same conditions, helping you get a comprehensive view of forecasts.

Responding to Winter Weather Warnings

When you receive a winter warning, it's essential to act quickly to ensure your safety and the safety of those around you. Here's a step-by-step approach to dealing with each level of warning:

Check Alerts Frequently: For ongoing severe weather, check alerts frequently as conditions can change rapidly. If you receive a yellow or amber warning, monitor the situation closely.

Assess Your Plans: If you're planning to travel, especially on long trips, consider postponing or rerouting to avoid the worst of the weather. For high-impact warnings, avoid travel altogether if possible.

Prepare Your Home and Car: Take time to weatherproof your home, ensuring windows, doors, and pipes are protected from freezing temperatures. If you must travel, make sure your car has an emergency kit, including blankets, a flashlight, water, and food.

Stay in Contact: Let family members and friends know about your plans. Share your travel routes and check in with someone regularly if you're going to be on the road during severe weather.

Follow Official Advice: For red warnings, take the highest level of precaution, as these conditions can pose serious risks. Follow any evacuation orders or safety recommendations issued by local authorities.

Chapter 3: How Snow and Winter Conditions Impact Daily Life

Chapter Overview

Snow and winter weather affect more than just the landscape—they shape daily life in significant ways. This chapter will cover how cold weather influences essential services, travel, and daily routines, and provide practical tips to help you adapt and stay safe.

1. Transportation and Travel

Road Safety: Snow and icy conditions increase the risk of accidents and travel delays, especially in regions unaccustomed to significant snowfall. It's vital to slow down, maintain a safe distance from other vehicles, and avoid sudden braking.

Public Transport: Rail and bus services may experience delays or cancellations due to snow or ice on the tracks and roads. Checking transport updates and allowing extra travel time is essential during winter weather alerts.

Flight Delays and Cancellations: Snow and ice often lead to flight disruptions, particularly at smaller airports without extensive de-icing resources. Preparing for possible delays by booking flexible travel options or travel insurance can help avoid complications.

2. Power Outages and Utility Services

Cold Weather Power Demand: Winter temperatures increase the demand for electricity, especially for heating. Power outages can occur due to high demand or storms disrupting lines. Stocking up on essentials and having backup light sources (like flashlights or candles) can be crucial in these situations.

Water Pipes and Heating Systems: Freezing temperatures may cause water pipes to burst, especially in older buildings. Insulating pipes, keeping indoor temperatures steady, and knowing where the main water valve is located can prevent extensive damage and inconvenience.

3. Health and Safety Considerations

Hypothermia and Frostbite: Cold temperatures put people at risk of hypothermia and frostbite, particularly the elderly, children, and those without sufficient heating. Wearing layered clothing, limiting time outdoors, and ensuring homes are well-heated can help prevent these issues.

Mental Well-being: Limited sunlight and extended indoor time can impact mental health, leading to seasonal affective disorder (SAD) and feelings of isolation. Taking short outdoor walks, staying connected with loved ones, and maintaining indoor lighting can support mental well-being during darker months.

4. Grocery Shopping and Essentials

Stocking Up: Snowy conditions can disrupt food supply chains, especially in rural areas. Planning ahead by keeping basic groceries and essentials at home is a good safety measure.

Emergency Supplies: It's wise to keep a supply of winter essentials, like non-perishable food, bottled water, blankets, and a basic first-aid kit, especially in areas where heavy snow could lead to temporary isolation.

Key Takeaways

Winter conditions affect multiple aspects of daily life, from travel and utilities to health and safety.

Proactively adapting routines and preparing emergency supplies can help individuals manage the challenges of snow and cold weather more effectively.

Chapter 4: Staying Safe in Severe Winter Conditions

Chapter Overview

This chapter offers essential tips for staying safe during extreme winter weather, from staying warm to avoiding common hazards caused by snow and ice. Whether you're at home, on the road, or outdoors, understanding these safety strategies can reduce risks.

1. Staying Warm Indoors

Home Heating: Keep your home's thermostat at a comfortable, steady temperature, and consider using space heaters in frequently used areas. Make sure to follow safety guidelines for all heating devices.

Preventing Heat Loss: Closing blinds or curtains at night, sealing any draughty windows, and using door stoppers can help retain warmth. Layering blankets and wearing indoor winter clothing can also make a difference in comfort.

2. Outdoor Precautions

Dressing for Cold Weather: Wear multiple layers, with the innermost layer made of moisture-wicking material to keep dry. Waterproof, insulated boots and gloves are crucial for outdoor comfort and warmth.

Avoiding Icy Surfaces: Walking on ice increases the risk of falls. Wear shoes with good traction, walk carefully, and, if possible, use salt or sand to reduce slipping risks on paths and driveways.

3. Travel Safety Tips

Preparing Your Vehicle: Ensure that your car is winter-ready by checking the battery, tires, and antifreeze levels. Keep an emergency kit with blankets, snacks, a flashlight, and first-aid essentials in your vehicle.

Driving in Snow and Ice: If travel is unavoidable, drive at reduced speeds, increase your following distance, and avoid sudden stops. It's always best to delay travel if possible when severe snow or ice warnings are in effect.

4. Handling Power Outages

Backup Heat Sources: If the power goes out, have backup heating methods like a portable heater (follow safety guidelines) or a wood-burning fireplace. Dress warmly and stay in a single room to conserve warmth.

Keeping Food Safe: Limit refrigerator and freezer door openings to keep food cold for as long as possible. Stocking non-perishable food items can also be helpful in case of extended outages.

Key Takeaways

Staying warm and taking precautions outdoors and in your vehicle can reduce winter-related risks.

Preparing for potential power outages by having a backup plan is key to staying safe and comfortable during winter weather events.

Chapter 5: How to Prepare for Snow and Freezing Temperatures

Chapter Overview

This chapter focuses on preparation tips for households, neighborhoods, and communities to effectively manage the effects of snow and freezing temperatures. Being proactive about winter readiness can make a significant difference when severe weather hits.

1. Preparing Your Home

Insulating Windows and Doors: Draft-proofing your home by sealing gaps around windows and doors can prevent heat from escaping and reduce heating costs.

Protecting Pipes: Frozen pipes can lead to bursts and costly repairs. Insulate any exposed pipes and consider allowing a small drip of water from faucets during particularly cold nights to prevent freezing.

Roof and Gutter Maintenance: Clear gutters to prevent ice buildup, which can cause leaks and other damage. If you have concerns about snow load on your roof, consider hiring a professional to help with snow removal.

2. Stocking Essentials

Food and Water: Keep at least a few days' supply of non-perishable foods and bottled water. This can be helpful if travel becomes difficult or stores temporarily close.

Medicine and Emergency Supplies: Have enough medication and first-aid supplies on hand. An emergency kit with flashlights, batteries, blankets, and a portable phone charger is also recommended.

3. Community Safety

Helping Vulnerable Neighbours: Check in with elderly neighbours or those with mobility challenges to ensure they have essentials and warmth.

Shared Resources: Coordinate with neighbours to share resources, such as snow-clearing equipment or supplies, to help each other manage the effects of severe weather more effectively.

4. Pet and Animal Safety

Outdoor Animal Shelters: Ensure that any outdoor animals have adequate shelter, food, and water. Regularly check for frozen water sources and consider bringing animals indoors if possible.

Pet Preparedness: For household pets, make sure to have enough food, any necessary medications, and a warm place for them to rest during extreme cold.

Key Takeaways

Preparing your home, stocking supplies, and coordinating with neighbours are essential steps in managing winter weather challenges.

Looking out for others and ensuring the safety of pets and animals strengthens community resilience during harsh winter conditions.